Enough Is Enough!

Transform Yourself & Find the Freedom to Love

By Lise Lavigne

Copyright © 2016 Lise Lavigne
All Rights Reserved.
Unauthorized duplication or distribution is strictly prohibited.

ISBN-13: 978-0-9970968-2-8
ISBN-10: 0-9970968-2-9

Published by: Celebrity Expert Author
http://celebrityexpertauthor.com

Canadian Address:
501- 1155 The High Street,
Coquitlam, BC, Canada
V3B.7W4
Phone: (604) 941-3041
Fax: (604) 944-7993

US Address:
1300 Boblett Street
Unit A-218
Blaine, WA 98230
Phone: (866) 492-6623
Fax: (250) 493-6603

TABLE OF CONTENTS

Preface... 1

Introduction... 5

Element #1: *Develop The Trust That Looking Deep Inside Yourself Will Not Hurt You*............. 7

Element #2: *Let Yourself See The Events That Hurt Or Disempowered You; Let The Feelings Flow* .. 29

Element #3: *Clear the Stuff that Keeps You from Being Who You Really Are; Forgive*........... 47

Element #4: *Discover Who You Really Are; Start Loving Yourself*............................. 63

Element #5: *Build The Life You Want From a Place of Freedom & Self-Love* 79

Conclusion 93

Resources...97

PREFACE

This book that you have in your hands right now could save your life. Women who are in abusive relationships often don't leave, even though they want to, and may feel powerless or unable to change. But there is hope. You will find that this book is like Pandora's mythical box: as you go through the steps to become a strong, empowered woman who controls her own life and has the self-worth to protect herself from danger, you will uncover a lot of emotions from the past, including some that you don't want to experience. But like Pandora's box, what also comes with this is one very important thing: hope. Hope for a better future, hope for a life in which you are not afraid of the ones with whom you spend the most time, and hope for a happier, healthier, more genuine you.

Think back to a time when you were the happiest. What kind of person were you then? What activities were you involved in? Who were the people around you? Maybe you haven't felt that happy for a long time, but it's never too late to bring back that happiness and goodness that once surrounded you. No matter what has happened to you or what mistakes you may have made in your life, you can always change. I hope to be able to support you through your transformational journey as you let go of abusive relationships or forgive those who have hurt you in the past, discover who you really are once you are living life for yourself, and embrace your inherent talents and goodness.

Before you put this book back on the shelf, realize that this could be your one chance to turn your life around. You know you're worth more than you admit to yourself. Deep down, you know that you have infinite worth, just as all other living beings have. Consider this book your life raft, safely transporting you across a stormy ocean to the safety of the shore. Words have power, and I can honestly tell you that not too long ago, I was in your shoes. I didn't think I could love myself. I didn't care about my life or what happened to me. But something changed inside of me, and I want to share that with you in this book.

Give me the chance to help you to transform yourself, your relationships, and your life. You don't ever have to go back to someone who will not treat you with respect or kindness. Nobody ever deserves to be abused or threatened. Please seek help through other resources if you are currently in an abusive relationship. (If your life is currently in danger, please turn to the "Resources" page at the back of this book to get the phone number and website of women's shelters, where you can stay until you're able to get into a safer situation on your own. You will also find phone numbers and websites for suicide crisis lines.)

Throughout this book, I will do my best to teach you how to take back ownership of your life and live a life that you can be proud of. These five critical elements will guide you in your transformation as you find your freedom to love:

- Element #1: Develop the trust that looking deep inside yourself will not hurt you

- Element #2: Let yourself see the events that hurt or disempowered you; let the feelings flow

- Element #3: Clear the stuff that keeps you from being who you really are; forgive

- Element #4: Discover who you really are; start loving yourself

- Element #5: Build the life you want from a place of freedom & self-love

Read on to learn exactly how to transform yourself and find the freedom to love.

INTRODUCTION

I never thought I could feel powerful in my whole life. I never thought I could affect people in the way I affect them. I never thought my little life would make a big difference in somebody else's life.

I'm a poor little girl from Ottawa, who barely had enough to eat and clothes to wear, who was abused in different ways, felt unloved and unwanted. I was an accident; I was supposed to be aborted. So many people have hurt me in my life in all the ways you can imagine. I was nobody.

I felt useless and good-for-nothing, but that was an illusion. It wasn't the real me at all. This is the real me, the way I am now. I'm so different than what I used to be. I'm so happy now. I have purpose, I love people, and I love life. It's so wonderful seeing that I can make a difference.

The past doesn't hurt me anymore. Nobody hurts me. I've decided to choose this life. You can make your life however you want it to be; you really can. You just have to believe it and change a few things in your head.

I want to tell all of the women who try to please others and who are always judging themselves how to stop doing that. My advice is to sit down, and whatever doesn't feel right, don't do any more. If part of you inside says, "No, I shouldn't be doing that," then just don't do it.

When you stop trying to be the person that you think you should be and just be the person that you are, then you stop hearing the voice in your head and you are free to trust and love people. You get the love you've always wanted. When you're genuine about who you are, you prepare the way to have anything you want.

Throughout this book, we will be using a simple format to address each of the questions and concerns you will have about learning to forgive and love yourself to open the doors to good, healthy relationships and build your self-worth. This book is made up of five elements; in each element, there are steps to follow and detailed attributes that will guide you through the process of becoming emotionally free. Becoming happy with yourself gives you control over your life; isn't it time that you cared about yourself?

ELEMENT #1:
Develop The Trust That Looking Deep Inside Yourself Will Not Hurt You

> "Trust that, when you are not holding yourself together so tightly, you will not fall apart. Trust that it is more important to fulfill your authentic desires than listen to your fears. Trust that your intuition is leading you somewhere. Trust that the flow of life contains you, is bigger than you, and will take care of you—if you let it."
>
> —Vironika Tugaleva (author of *The Love Mindset*)

Welcome to the first critical element of personal transformation. This element is all about trusting that looking deep inside of yourself will not hurt you. In step #1, you will discover what currently brings you feelings of self-worth. In step #2, you will contemplate why you believe those things determine your self-worth. Step #3 is where you will question whether you are being your best, genuine self, which is key to accepting and loving yourself. Next, in step #4, you will consider who you would be if you let go of negative thoughts and beliefs about who you are or who you can be. Finally, step #5 will guide you in no longer sacrificing yourself for the sake of winning others' attention.

This book is ideal for women who want to change their lives for the better. Critical element #1, "Develop the Trust That Looking Deep Inside Yourself Will Not Hurt You," is your personal guide to gaining the best perspective on who you really are. We will be following these five steps throughout this first element:

- Step #1: Ask yourself what things make you good
- Step #2: Ask yourself why you think these things make you good
- Step #3: Ask yourself, "Is this really me?"
- Step #4: Find out who you would be without bad thoughts
- Step #5: Decide to stop making the sacrifice

Step #1: Ask Yourself What Things Make You Good

Before you've created new beliefs in your mind about yourself and the world around you, you should ask yourself what things make you good. What is it that defines your goodness as a person? (Later in this book, we will find out what really makes you good.)

Your Physical Appearance

One of the most common things that people think make

them good is this first supporting attribute: your physical appearance. When somebody is hooked on their physical appearance to feel good, they will do anything to look good, even if it means spending money they don't have or buying clothing that they don't like.

This vanity encourages people to always be comparing themselves to models and celebrities at their best (after a team of makeup artists, hair stylists, and professional photographers have done their work), which is an unrealistic standard. Just look at the difference between the "before and after" pictures of various celebrities who have been PhotoShopped to look better; there is no way that anyone could naturally have skin that flawless or look that amazing in real life.

By focusing on your flaws and shortcomings, you are essentially encouraging yourself to be dissatisfied with your body and yourself—especially when you see your goodness as being dependent on your physical appearance. If your body shape is not perfect (you're overweight, too skinny, or not muscular enough), you're always focusing on that, even if your ideal is impossible to achieve.

Your physical appearance is not what really makes you good. You shouldn't have to put all of your makeup on before you can even leave the house to grab the newspaper, or get distracted during conversations because you're worrying that the other person doesn't like your hair, or fear the gym because you think you're too fat or wimpy and everyone will judge you.

Stop wasting your time comparing yourself to others. If you have to compare, then compare how healthy you are now to how healthy (or unhealthy) you have been in the past. Your body doesn't determine whether people will love you. Your body doesn't determine whether you can be successful in life or not. You don't have to meet anyone else's standards of beauty; embrace yourself as you are and decide to love yourself no matter what, because you are more than your body, you are more than your flaws, and as a human being, you have an inherent worth that is beyond measure.

Stop believing that your external appearance is a mirror of your inner goodness, because that simply isn't true. You are good because of who you are, not because of what you look like.

Making Other People Happy

If you're trying to make other people happy, it will be to your own detriment if you're not being true to yourself. Always trying to please other people and never yourself is not a healthy way of living, and it just doesn't work, especially if you end up doing things that are wrong or hurting yourself because all you care about is pleasing the other person.

Never putting yourself first makes you feel as though you're worth less than others, and instead of making other people happy and loving them, you might find yourself resenting them. For example, you might think, "I do all of these things—I cook, I clean, I always try to say the right thing and act the right way—and they don't even notice!"

By learning to love yourself first, rather than focusing on winning someone over all the time, you won't have to do those things. Instead, you will naturally become the kind of person who others enjoy being around, and you can be loved that way. Trying too hard to be someone else's ideal person just pushes them away and makes both of you value yourself less. Be your own person.

Doing Things You Don't Want to Make Someone Else Happy

There are a number of ways that people try to please others. Sometimes it's as simple as saying things that you think they want to hear (whether what you're saying is true or not), while other times, you might even put your values and beliefs aside to conform to what you think they want. You might start smoking because they smoke and you think they don't like non-smokers, or start drinking because they think it's fun, even though you don't want to smoke or drink.

Or you might dress a certain way because you think that person will like you more because of it, but then if you hang out with a different set of friends or a new significant other, then you dress another kind of way to please *that* group, or your romantic interest. The same goes for your personality and how you act; you might find yourself feeling like an imposter because you're never who you really are, since you think that nobody will like you as you are.

However, if you're not pleasing yourself—if you're not dressing the way you like, acting the way you like, and making lifestyle choices based on your own values—and you're doing it to please other people, at the end of the day you feel guilty. You think, "Oh, man, why did I do that? I didn't want to do that," and you're not happy because you're not pleasing yourself in a healthy way.

In the end, you have a choice: will you continue living somebody else's life, scrambling to keep up with what you think other people want from you, hoping that they will love you? Or will you live your own life independent of what you perceive others want, and gain emotional freedom that allows you to love someone in a healthy way, and be loved by others for who you are?

It's an easy choice once you realize that you can never keep up with others' expectations; instead, you must create your own standards for yourself and follow them instead. Relying on others to tell you how to live your life will only prevent you from living your best life; whether you're drinking, doing drugs, spending money you don't have, or engaging in other unhealthy behaviors to try to win someone's love, you will eventually realize that this life is yours to live. Live for yourself. The love that you want from others will come naturally when you're true to yourself and you're making yourself happy, which makes it easy for others to be happy when they're around you.

Never Thinking of Pleasing Yourself

Never pleasing yourself is a very common problem for many women, especially with the pressure to have children and be the one who takes care of the entire household. Many women put themselves last because they just want to please the other people around them and do what they want. It's safer, because you never have to address what's really going on with yourself; you just shove those emotions away and focus on trying to please others, even if it means doing something you don't want to do. When you're doing this, you're hiding your personality and not having the courage to be true to yourself. That hurts you because if you're not yourself, then who are you?

The cost of not being yourself is that you feel like you're an imposter. You can feel resentment towards others even though they're not the ones who decided you have to do everything you can to please them, because you're giving them much more than what you're getting out of the relationship. It's an emotional imbalance that didn't even need to be there.

Fortunately, it's never too late to change. You don't have to be a slave to fear anymore; take the courage to be yourself and know that you are good enough. Living up to someone else's standards (whether real or assumed) isn't necessary; people really will love you the way you really are if you have the courage to show your true self to them.

When you're not being yourself, you sometimes feel so much anger, guilt, and discouragement that you just want to quit these people. You just want to abandon them or get into verbal arguments with them. That's a sign that the real you wants to come out. Don't be fearful anymore. Have the courage to be yourself, despite what others may think of you.

Step #2: Ask Yourself Why You Think These Things Make You Good

It's Good to Make Other People Happy

Early in my life, I learned that it's good to make other people happy, even if it didn't make me happy. I was a child when I had to start doing things I didn't want to do, by touching others in certain ways or allowing them to touch me in a certain way. I let them do things to my body that would not have been allowed, but I was too young to know that it was wrong.

Over time, coming from that background of having been abused, you believe that it's good to make other people happy, even if it hurts you. When I was a child, there was a man in my family who I was supposed to trust and love, who was supposed to love and protect me. When he said, "Can you do this to me? It's going to feel really good and I'll like it, and you'll like it, too. Don't you want to make me happy?" I went along with it. Just by doing it, I subconsciously believed at three or four years old that, "Well, he should know better, because he's older, so I'll do it to make him happy. It's okay to do this." But it's wrong; the whole thing is wrong.

Maybe you experienced something similar that taught you to put others before you. Even if you had a good, healthy upbringing in which you were safe, maybe you watched your mother take care of everyone except herself and internalized that belief, or for whatever other reason, you simply decided that you weren't good enough and that you had to meet others' ideals in order to be loved.

In this book, we will find out how to overcome this incorrect mindset and learn how to gain the emotional freedom that allows us to have good, healthy, strong relationships with others in which we respect ourselves and others, and there are clearly defined boundaries that are also respected.

Learning to Be Good as a Child

My childhood changed my mindset; I learned to please people, even when that meant doing things that were wrong. I did what I thought others wanted just to try to please them. My belief was that it didn't matter how I felt or what I said or what I did, as long as it was something that somebody I loved wanted me to do. I thought I should do anything that they expected or seemed to expect from me so that they would get some happiness out of it.

The truth is, though, that unless you are good to yourself,

you cannot really be good to others. If you're unhappy, others around you will pick up on that, even if you're trying to be happy for them. Without that emotional footing to rely on, where you're taking good care of yourself and remembering that even if the entire world were against you, you would still love yourself and you would still be deserving of that love, it just doesn't work.

We all learned things from our upbringing and life experiences, but sometimes, you learn the wrong thing and you have to let go of that wrong belief. Letting go of those beliefs is part of what gives you the emotional release that makes room for the good feelings to come into your life, and you can then build up good, strong beliefs about what life is really like and how you should live.

Learning How to Make the People You Love Happy

Your childhood shapes how you will live as an adult. I learned to want to make people happy, even if it didn't make me happy. I saw this in other people, too; my sister told our mother about something that happened, and our mother didn't believe her, so to make her happy, my sister lied and said, "Well, I was lying. It never happened." But it did happen, and my sister knew that.

When all you do is try to make others happy, you give up your own values and boundaries. Everything becomes okay, even if it's something bad that hurts you, because you're never standing up for yourself and telling others no. You even start lying because you want to make that person who you love happy by saying, "Okay, well, it didn't really happen," or "It was my fault." All you're focusing on are things that make others happy, which leads you to lie about anything that other people don't want to hear, even if it's important.

Seeking to Be Loved More

Feeling like you need to make the people you love feel happy, at any cost, even if that means lying or not making yourself happy becomes a trap, because other people dictate what makes them happy, and you carry that out without question. When you're caught in this trap, you're always seeking to be loved because you don't feel loved inside or you aren't loved at all. Many people could actually love you, but even if it's there, you don't feel that love; you just have an empty feeling inside, a void. That emptiness pushes you to always be searching for something that might already be there, but you can't see it right in front of you. So you decide to keep looking for love.

It could be your friends who you seek love from; when you're growing up, you try different crowds of people, and sometimes it's the wrong crowd. But sometimes that's the only crowd that you feel loved in, so you hang out with them anyway. It could be a crowd of smokers, drug users, or partiers, and then your need for love becomes insatiable; you're wanting to feel loved, so you're always trying to get that feeling of being loved, but you're never getting it.

That leaves you never feeling good enough. You're always thinking that you're the ugly duckling, even if you're not, or always the odd man out, even if that's not completely true. You're home alone with your thoughts, and you're always thinking, "Nobody loves me. I'm not pretty like them," but it's not true. Or, "I don't talk the way they talk, I don't think the way they think, and I'm not good in school like they are."

You're always comparing yourself to everybody else, and you just don't like yourself at all. Sometimes, it can be so bad that you just want to end your life; you think you don't belong on this earth. I tried to kill myself three times because of that feeling that there just wasn't enough love for me, so I know what it's like. It doesn't have to be this way. Realizing this can give you hope when you're struggling with this cycle of pleasing others to try to win them over.

Step #3: Ask Yourself, "Is This Really Me?"

When Things You Do Don't Make You Happy

You're still at the point where the things that you're doing to seek love don't make you happy, because you're doing them for someone else, not for yourself. This cycle of doing things that don't make you happy only worsens your unhappiness, because not only are you missing out on doing things that do make you happy, but you're also doing things you don't really want to do—and for a lost cause, because you can never make someone love you. Whether other people love you or not is outside of your control.

This sadness might not be obvious to you, but when you experience it, you will feel like something is missing in life. Nothing really makes you laugh anymore, or you do laugh and be rowdy sometimes, but most of the time, you're not feeling joyful inside. And that's from not listening to your gut feeling. You feel like there's a voice inside that says, "No, you don't like those clothes; why aren't you wearing what you like? These shoes are not comfortable at all; why are you wearing those 5-inch high heels when you want to wear running shoes? Why are you trying to smoke when you don't like the taste of it, or even the look of it?" That's the voice that you should be listening to, because it's encouraging you to be who you really are, not who everyone else wants or expects you to be.

Should You Be Doing This?

Sometimes, you just have to take time out to be alone with your thoughts, and just start listening. Find out what you should and shouldn't be doing; pay attention to how your choices make you feel. For example, what happens when you start saying no to things that you normally wouldn't want to do? Take some time to ponder whether you should be doing what you're doing. Then, when the time comes to decide, you will already know what choice you should make.

That Feeling Inside of You That Says "No"

Starting to say "no" to people is hard. It's tough to start saying, "No, I'm sorry; I don't really want to do that," "No, I'm going to wear this outfit instead," or, "No, I'm sorry; I'm not going to go drinking with you." Or, "No..." You have to start somewhere; whatever it is that you really don't want to do, just don't do it. Even if you just say "no" to one thing that you don't want to do, you'll feel so good about that. You'll think, "Oh my gosh! I said 'no'! And it's not the end of the world!"

Once you say "no" to one thing, you get the courage to say "no" to another thing, and another thing, until you're only ever saying "yes" to the things that you actually want to do. You'll see that it's not that hard, and you'll begin to define the person that's really you.

When I began saying "no" to people and to the things that

I didn't want to do or that wasn't me, I was saying "no" to fear. That's when you realize, "Oh my goodness, I did this! I said 'no,' and none of the bad things that I thought would happen actually happened." Although you might not notice an immediate difference when you first start saying "no" to things that you don't want to do, it will bring you more freedom and happiness, and you will feel more powerful and confident. It's an amazing feeling to be able to assert your boundaries and say "no" to things you don't want to do.

The Cost of Not Being Yourself

The cost of not being you is missing out on your life, missing out on so much more happiness, and experiencing the bad things that come from saying "yes" when you should be saying "no" (such as activities that breed guilt, fear, and resentment).

When you are true to yourself, those bad feelings aren't there at the end of the day, or even throughout the day; instead of feeling self-pity, powerlessness, or like you want to hide, you're being true to yourself and you're taking charge of your own life.

As you start doing what you want to do, you can realize, "Wow! I did this good thing; look! And nobody hurt me. I can still be myself, and nothing bad comes from this."

Step #4: Find Out Who You Would Be Without Bad Thoughts

Develop the Courage to Be Able to Say "No"

Everyone has courage within themselves. You don't need to

wait to be someone who is courageous; that courage is already there, just waiting to be used. So be courageous by telling yourself, "Okay, I can do this. I'm going to establish my boundaries."

Letting others dictate your life won't bring you happiness, and you know it. If you don't want to go out drinking with your friends, don't go. Use your courage to say, "No, I'm not going out tonight; I want to stay home." This is particularly important whenever it's something that isn't going to be healthy for you—drinking, drugs, or otherwise harming your body.

When you're saying "yes" to others' demands and you're conforming to them, in a twisted way, it's almost as if you're manipulating them. You're trying to change them, because you can see that they're not happy, but you don't realize you have no control over them. They can change themselves if that's what they really want, and you can change yourself if that's what you really want, but you cannot make someone else change. Once you stop trying to change them, you're taking your life back. You're focusing your efforts on the things that you can control: your own behavior.

Change your own life, and you won't need to change them. If they're dragging you down, you can let go of that unhealthy relationship and find someone who will lift you up and encourage you to be yourself, as well as support you in what you're doing with your life.

This Isn't Me

When you start saying "no" to all of the things that aren't you, it definitely starts to show you who you really are. By saying "no" to what you don't want, you make room for the things that you do want, that bring peace and happiness to your life.

Drawing the line makes you feel more confident and powerful. Those bad feelings of guilt and shame that come from not being true to yourself will go away, and the good things that start to happen will bring good feelings instead: peace, joy, happiness, and contentment. You start feeling like your real self.

As the real you starts to show itself, you will actually feel like a different person, and the person who you were living as all of your life disappears slowly but surely as you embrace who you really are instead. Sometimes, this transformation happens quickly; I think it happened pretty quickly in my case, and it just feels so much better to be myself now. I see life with such a better perspective, I see people in a better light, and I have more love for them,instead of fearing that I won't be good enough for them.

The Freedom You Get from Not Worrying about Losing Somebody

In the past, I would do anything to not lose a relationship with someone, especially somebody who I loved, and I would try all kinds of different things to please them. I was afraid to lose them, so I would rely on doing everything I could to please them, even if it meant harming myself in the process. But once I was no longer afraid of losing them, once I was free to be myself, that's when my belief shifted to, "Oh, well, if these people don't like the real me, then I'm not going to hang around them. It's not important."

That's because I had started to live as myself. Once I started to say "no" to things that I didn't want in my life, I had more room to be who I am today: my true, genuine self. And I loved myself more because of it.

The next time you look in the mirror, don't waste time criticizing your imperfections. I tell myself, "Well, you don't look like Catherine Zeta-Jones, but you're just different. You're beautiful in your own way." When you start loving yourself more, you really don't care anymore if you are loved by every single person in your life. You love yourself even if they don't.

As you start to take these little steps, such as saying "no" to things that aren't you or that would harm you, you will learn how to be true to yourself and protect yourself. Then, naturally, you will be able to get over this fear of losing people. You won't worry as much about pleasing others, because you know that they are the only ones who can ultimately make themselves happy, and it's your job to make yourself happy. That starts with loving yourself.

If It Doesn't Make You Happy & You Think It's Wrong, It Imprisons You

By constantly trying to please others and ignoring their own needs, people create a prison for themselves in which they cannot be themselves. Focusing only on what makes others happy, talking about bad things, and neglecting yourself imprisons you. If you live your life by pleasing other people, you will feel like you're in a prison, because you don't get to do what you really, really want to do, which stops you from living your life fully. It stops you from being happy, because you're always thinking of different ways to please others, but never yourself.

It's as if you lose yourself in the process, because all of the people in your life are so different from one another, which means they have varying expectations of you, and what one likes, another doesn't, and so forth. You get caught in the trap of behaving one way around one person, and a completely different way around a different person, and then... what on earth do you do when both of them are with you at the same time, and you cannot please one without risking neglecting what the other wants?

You can just drive yourself crazy worrying about what everyone else thinks and wants: oh, you can't drink with that person, but this person likes champagne, and that person likes beer, and you hate beer so the closest you come is by drinking a cider or something. Or, some people expect you to dress casually, another group of people all wear Gucci or Prada...

When everything in your life is dependent upon what another person or another group of people want, you run around in circles trying to be everything to everyone, and it just doesn't work. It just drives you absolutely nuts! Once you take control of your life and do whatever you want that pleases yourself, not the crowd you hang out with or your co-workers or your parents or anyone else, this insanity finally stops. You can finally do just one thing, and that thing is to please yourself.

Step #5:   Decide to Stop Making the Sacrifice

It's not worth it. Stop making the sacrifice.

Finally Waking Up

To wake up from this, I had to say, "Enough is enough! Enough is enough, and I don't know how you're going to do it, but you're just going to do one small thing to change."

When you wake up and you stop doing all of the things that you were doing to please other people, the real you starts to emerge. People start to see you with different eyes. Although some of them might abandon you, it doesn't really matter, because they weren't your real friends anyway because you couldn't be yourself with them.

Some people start to say, "Oh, I love this new you! What happened?!" And you realize, "Oh my goodness, I didn't even have to please these people! I've wasted all of this time when I could have just been myself, and they would have still been there for me!" That gives you the best feeling, knowing that you can be yourself with your friends.

Wake Up & Ask Yourself, "What Am I Doing?"

When you finally wake up, you will experience that moment of realization: "What am I doing? I can be myself, and people will still like me." If some people don't like you, that's okay; it doesn't matter, because you're attracting more people to you just by being yourself. When you're at work or walking down the street, more and more people will come to your life—and the people who were already there will love you more because you're being genuine. Anyone who leaves you weren't meant to be there to begin with, because those people were just hurting you by only wanting you to be someone you're not.

Enough Is Enough!

Eventually, after being hurt so much in life, you finally reach bottom, and that's it. You can't take any more of this pain, so you say, "Enough is enough! It's just too painful to go on like this!" Something has to change, and you know it.

To get to that point, you have to start realizing where this ns all coming from. Sit down quietly and start figuring out how it all began.

Some of us have been hurting from the time that we were little, when somebody did something bad to us. If that happened to you, then you have to face it. You don't have to blame anybody, but you have to go back to the beginning if you want to start over and see how your life should be instead.

Once you're back there, you can see what went wrong. Which incorrect or harmful beliefs have you internalized that you have no use for anymore? How can you replace those beliefs with something that will help you on your life's journey from now on? Sometimes, all you have to do is realize that you began believing the wrong thing (such as that unless you're perfect, nobody will ever really love you), and then take some time to decide what you will believe instead (such as that you are loved, and you don't need to be perfect or meet a near-perfect standard to feel loved).

Just Don't Do This to Begin With

The easiest cure is to not need a cure. Just don't do what you feel isn't right. Free your mind from negative thoughts or from beliefs that aren't serving you.

Everybody has an inner "voice" or gut feeling, which you might think of as your intuition, that guides you. That's what tells you, "Don't do that!" when you're about to do something you would regret. It's there to protect us, but many people ignore it or think that it won't make a difference, like an alcoholic who has one drink and then thinks it's too late so they just keep drinking.

But you don't have to keep doing the wrong thing, even if

you ignored your intuitive feeling and made the wrong choice. At any point in your life, whether it's a big thing or a small thing, you can turn things around and say, "No more of this. I'm going to make good choices from now on."

When you start listening to your intuition, it gives you protection. Following your intuition is one of the keys to freedom. Often, we ignore those red flags, those feelings that tell us not to do what we're doing, and we assign all kinds of excuses to ignore it, because we're so focused on pleasing another person. But when you start listening to that inner voice, you can start saying "no" to the bad things that come your way and that aren't you. You can use your courage to take back your power and set yourself free.

Element #1 Conclusion

Take the time to consider what you have learned in this element before moving on to the next one. Go for a short walk, preferably in nature, and let it all sink in. There's no need to rush; it's perfectly normal and natural for your emotional journey to take time.

As you continue learning how to see the situation you are in, heal from the past, and move forward to better days, do what you can to reduce your stress level so you will have optimal results. Don't be afraid to delegate tasks to your co-workers, say "no" to hosting a dinner party that you're not very interested in, or ask your partner or friends for help.

Get enough sleep, drink plenty of water, eat your veggies, and do whatever you think you can reasonably do to live healthier. If you only make one change while going through this process, it should be to give yourself the time to relax and think about what you're learning in this book.

The next element in this book will guide you through looking back at the past and experiencing the emotions that you have shut away for so long.

Go to www.LiseLavigne.com/worksheets to download your Compassionate Reality Check Worksheet before you continue reading.

ELEMENT #2:
Let Yourself See The Events That Hurt Or Disempowered You; Let The Feelings Flow

> "The more you trust your intuition, the more empowered you become, the stronger you become, and the happier you become."
>
> —Gisele Bündchen (model, actress, & producer)

Welcome to the second critical element of personal transformation. This element is all about learning to love yourself and letting yourself feel the suppressed emotions that you have been holding onto for years or even your whole life.

In step #6, you will start to see yourself the way that a benevolent, unconditionally loving being sees you. In step #7, you will stop trying to control everything and, instead, allow life to happen naturally and see the good even in the difficulties. Step #8 is where you will finally release the emotions that had been blocking your progress in life. Take a breath before beginning step #9, in which you will embrace the space of pure acceptance in preparation for step #10, which will show you to look at your life so far and find out what is working and what needs to change.

This book is ideal for women who want to change their lives for the better. Critical element #2, "Let Yourself See the Events That Hurt or Disempowered You; Let the Feelings Flow," is your personal guide to embracing yourself (both literally and in terms of self-acceptance; don't be afraid to give yourself a hug every now and then!). We will be following these five steps throughout this second element:

- Step #6: Discover who you would be without judgment
- Step #7: Throw your arms in the air and surrender to the forces you can't change
- Step #8: Let the pure emotions flow unobstructed
- Step #9: Enter the space of pure acceptance
- Step #10: See the events and circumstances of your life from a space of pure acceptance

Step #6: Discover Who You Would Be Without Judgment

Seeing yourself without judgment really allows you to see the events that hurt or disempowered you and let your feelings flow. We judge ourselves continually, and that self-judgment prevents us from being our real selves and being happy. To enter that space of non-judgment so that you can start to let the backed-up feelings flow, you have to love every part of yourself, even the parts of you that you haven't been loving.

Doing Things That You Don't Want to Do Makes You Feel Guilty

There are many things that we've carried over from the past because of our self-judgment, including guilt. The guilt makes us feel like we need to do things that we don't want to do and it makes you feel like you're an imposter. You just don't feel like yourself all the time, and you try to please more and more people. You feel guilty, you feel ashamed, and when you try to please people, it's like you're masking yourself. You try not to think about it, you try to get love, and you try to please others all the time, but you can see that it's not working, and you can feel it, too.

Pleasing Others Is a Trap That Makes You Feel Bad & Stupid

In trying to please other people to win them over and be loved, sometimes you're trying so much that it pushes them away. Maybe you care about them much more than they care about you, which makes them feel uncomfortable, or you spend money on them and they feel bad because you're spending too much money on them. You think you're pleasing them, because they mention that they need something, so you go to the store and buy it for them since you think that's what they want, but that's not really what they want.

So you've spent money that you didn't even have to begin with so that you can try to make them happy, but then it didn't even work. So they're not happy, you're not happy, you wasted your time and money, and you just feel bad about yourself because you think you're not good enough for them. What you're really craving is to be accepted and loved for who you really are, but this isn't the way to do it. You can't buy love, and you can't please people to make them love you. It just doesn't work.

Decide to Stop Judging Yourself

Decide to get over thinking that you're bad or that you're stupid. Think about all of the good things about you, and forget about the rest. Focus on being true to yourself.

If you spend money, you don't have to do it to please another person, because that's not going to help you. Dressing a certain way to please someone else means sacrificing part of the real you; if all you're concerned with is what others think, then you can't even behave like yourself because you're too worried about their own judgment of you.

Realize the Actions That You Can Stop Doing & Feel Better

Take the time to sit down quietly, alone with your thoughts. Bring a notepad and pen or pencil to make two lists. The first list should be all of the things that make you feel bad when you do them; that's your "stop doing this" list. The second list should be all of the things that make you feel good about yourself when you do them; that's your "start doing this" list.

You can take this a step further and make two more lists: the benefits and losses from what you're doing.

One of these lists should be the benefits that you and others get from your actions, including unexpected benefits, such as getting back in touch with a relative who you thought would never accept you for who you are.

The other list should be the losses that you and others get from your actions, including unexpected losses, such as spending all of your money on someone else—you might have thought it would benefit them and that you were pleasing them and showing your love for them, but you were actually pushing them away, or encouraging them to see you as little more than a source of money.

When you make these lists, you can see the real benefits of no longer spending money you don't need to spend, hanging out with a certain group of people, or doing something you don't want to do, whatever it is. Once you see where you need to change, you will be able to make those changes and feel truly happy because you're no longer doing things that make you feel guilty(and that you don't want to do anyway).

Ultimately, you want to feel happy and appreciated and loved for who you are. The truth is that you can't start loving other people until they appreciate who you really are. Making a list of things that make you feel happy, appreciated, and loved for who you are can give you something to focus on instead of seeking approval through pleasing other people.

Step #7: Throw Your Arms in the Air & Surrender to the Forces You Can't Change

Stop Pretending That It Doesn't Hurt

You have to really want to change before you're able to change; pretending that the bad things you're doing aren't hurting you, or that the people around you aren't negatively influencing you, only gets in the way of change. Don't waste your life away living in denial.

I've talked to so many people who think they're happy how

they are right now, but they're only 20-something. They don't think they're doing anything to make themselves unhappy. They really, really have to stop, but you have to have hit bottom to really want to change.

That's what happened to me: I was hurt so badly constantly that I had to say, "Okay, enough is enough! I'm not going to do this anymore!" I could not spend another day living in denial and pretending that the situation wasn't causing me pain.

Realize That Addictions Won't Help

When you're feeling lost and overwhelmed, you might suppress your feelings with drugs, alcohol, sex, or any other addictive behavior. You might not even be consciously aware of why you are doing that, but you're probably trying to mask or numb the pain, guilt, and shame that you just want to hide from yourself and everyone else.

The problem is that suppressing your feelings doesn't let you see the real cause of them, and those addictive behaviors can add to the difficulty of your situation.

You may engage in addictive behaviors because you feel different after drinking wine, doing drugs, going out and partying. You want to just forget, and you don't think you're addicted or that you could become addicted.

But that eventually leads to a rock-bottom moment where you say, "Okay, I'm not going to do this anymore. I don't know how to change, but I have to stop." Addictive behaviors are dangerous and difficult to quit; if you haven't already started smoking, drinking, or doing drugs, stay away from it. What you think is fun now can turn on you at any moment and become your worst nightmare. Nobody has ever said, "If only I had started drinking sooner," or "If only I had become a chain-smoker, my life really would have been great!"

Let the Pain Come; It's Okay to Cry

When you get real with yourself and come to terms with what you've been doing to yourself in your attempts to win the love of other people, you will really see a range of emotions. It's okay to sit down and cry for several minutes. It's okay to be angry and regretful. It's okay to be sad about all of the good things you've missed out on while engaging in bad behavior. Take your time to experience these pent-up emotions and stop suppressing them by drinking or distracting yourself in other unhealthy ways.

Let that pain come to the surface. It's better that it flows, because then you're not stuck with it sitting on your shoulders or pressing at your heart. Some people find it helpful to write down their feelings and vent that way; as Anna Nalick's song "Breathe" goes, "If I get it all down on paper, it's no longer inside of me, threatening the life it belongs to."

Maybe everything you've done so far hasn't done anything for you and you're still at the same point when you're 50! Your life hasn't improved in the ways that count; you might have luxury items, but it doesn't matter because of how you feel inside. You just think about those things that you've done, or should have done to prevent the pain, and the more you start thinking about it, the more you cry, because it didn't have to be that way. It didn't have to happen, but you allowed it to happen because you didn't know any better or you were too afraid or ashamed to protect yourself or even ask for help from someone else. All you wanted was to please people, and maybe you feel like your life fell apart even though you never thought that would happen because of it.

But you can't keep blaming yourself for the past, even if it was your fault. Whether it was your fault or someone else's fault or nobody's fault, you have to move on, because you can't stay chained to the past, wishing for some sort of miracle to happen where you can go back and do things differently. You can only change the things to come, not the things that have already happened. Set your sights on changing your future and living a good life in the present moment, not on regretting the past.

Somehow, You Know You Will Be Different on the Other Side

You know there's going to be a big, big difference once you're on the other side of this. You have to accept what has happened in your life, and know that it's not the real you. You can't pretend it didn't happen, but you can decide that it's not going to define you. You can decide to be a different person. Decide to be the real you.

Step #8:   Let the Pure Emotions Flow Unobstructed

Your Life Won't Change Overnight

It doesn't have to take a long time to change your life, because once you realize that what you've been doing isn't you, that's when you can adopt healthier behaviors instead in which you're being your true, genuine self.

Change won't happen overnight, but you will see it progress. Keep a journal or just make notes in a regular notebook to see how far you're progressing; you can write down whether you had a good day or not (why or why not?), whether you made choices that align with your true self, and you can see patterns of when you give in to peer pressure and when you have the courage to be independent of the crowd and make good choices.

To get this change started, you accept all of the things you've done and the things that have happened to you in the past. Decide, and remind yourself, "Okay, I can be a different person. I can be ME now."

You have to want this change, because if you don't want it, it's not going to happen. You have to want to stop the pain, and you stop the pain by no longer doing what's painful. It's as simple as that.

How You Feel Inside Will Change for the Better

By now, things are feeling different, almost instantaneously, because you've realized that pleasing other people regardless of what happens to you has to stop. You're not going to do this anymore; from this moment on, it's time that you make better decisions. Like if your boyfriend says, "Oh, why don't we go drinking at the club tonight?" you can say, "Oh, no, I'm sorry; I have a headache," or "I don't want to drink anymore. Let's go to a movie instead." Changing like that starts to build up your personal power. You're making better decisions and you avoid or take yourself out of bad situations.

Feel Peaceful as Your Heart Heals

Once you start letting the emotions flow, you can start allowing new emotions in, which are usually much better emotions. When you don't do the things you don't want to do, you do feel more peaceful about it and you feel more happy: "Oh, gosh, I said no! Usually, I would have said yes." When you start taking your life back, it's like the whole world is changing; you realize, "Oh, I can do this! I can just be me, and it's okay!"

The guilt and the shame that you always felt from saying "yes" to bad things stops taking up all the space in your heart. When you have room in your heart, the nicer feelings can come in. Better thoughts come in, you're alone with your own mind and you don't go around trying to please others, feeling guilt and shame as a result.

Instead, you live your own life and let others live their own lives. You're letting go of co-dependency, neediness, and the other types of emotional dysfunction that get in the way of healthy relationships. You'll see a positive difference, and so will those around you.

Have Hope for the New Path in Your Life

As you spend more time with yourself and think about what you would like to do, what you would like to be like, or what you would like to change for the better in your life, you feel more in control. That's what hope does for you: it opens up a whole new world where you can do whatever you want to do.

Without other people's expectations in the way, you have the freedom to achieve your aspirations. For example, you might decide, "I've always wanted to write a book; why don't I start writing?" And then instead of just thinking about how great it would be to become a published author, you schedule half an hour in the mornings and two hours in the evenings to work on your novel. Before you know it, you've achieved your goal, and you're so much happier—not just because you wrote a novel, but also because you did something for yourself.

The same thing goes for anything else you dream of doing. You start to think, "What if the things that I thought were impossible are actually possible? What if I write down my goals, make a plan, and actually do what I've always dreamed of doing?" Getting to this stage, you have to let go of control, even though it sounds like it's not logical, because that lets you give in to the emotions that haven't been expressed for so long. After you let the emotions flow and you've cried for what feels like hours, you have made room, emotionally, to start living a better life. And you know that you can do it.

Your world really does start to change. A new set of people come into your life, and you find nice people everywhere instead of attracting people who are abusive, who only want your body or your money or just like hanging out with you because you'll do whatever pleases them. You start to see that it is possible to go into a new space of being, and you go forward and actually do that.

Step #9:   Enter the Space of Pure Acceptance

By accepting what happened, you always have a choice and the opportunity to embrace bigger possibilities.

Trust in Something Bigger Than You

I believe we were created. I believe there's a Creator out there who made us. I believe in God. There are powers out there stronger than us.

When you trust in that bigger power and you don't have to

think that everything in your life is a result of you physically doing something, that you're not the one in charge of controlling everything, you have more hope. You can say, "Okay, I'll do the best that I can, and God is in charge. I don't have to explain it."

When you hope and you just trust, that's when you start to want better things, and you start attracting better things. I pray to God, I ask the Universe, God—I pray, I ask for what I want, and I believe that I'll get it. The more I've been asking, the more I've been getting. I don't want to say it's magic, because it's better than magic, really, because it's real!

There is a really big difference between the types of prayers you have when you're feeling guilty and shameful and you're all backed up with that emotion, versus the kind of prayer that you have once you enter a space of self-acceptance. When you feel guilt and shame, first of all, you don't want to pray; you don't want to talk to anybody, not even the God who made you. You can blame all of it on God, or you just stay away, and your prayers have fear, guilt, and shame in them. They're not prayers that will get you anywhere.

But when you're able to let go of those negative emotions and bring in all of the happiness, peace, love, and joy that you can experience in life, your prayers become much more sincere and positive. You know that God cares, because you can feel it.

Know That You Are Worthy

Knowing that you're worthy affects how you pray and how things happen in your life. That's because once you accept yourself and you're praying, you start appreciating the good things and feeling more hopeful. When you pray, you're more thankful. You might start out by saying, "I'm so thankful that you got me out of this mess," or "I'm so happy that I can feel your love for me."

By being more thankful, everything around you changes. Your beliefs about what you deserve change, because you know you're loved no matter what happens, and you know you have a purpose for being here. You become more bold, in a good way. You're being honest. You can dream all kinds of things.

For example, I love to write, and I want to write a book, and that's exactly what I'm doing now. I'm thinking, "Okay, I'm going to be a best-selling author!" I really believe that, because I can do it as much as anybody else, and I don't think that God has favorites. I can do it as much as any other person can. I'm just as smart as anybody else, even though I was told I was stupid all my life because I didn't go to university.

The same goes for you. You don't have to have a formal education to make a successful career. Some of the richest and most successful people in the world never graduated from college. They worked hard and did their own research on things that they needed to know for their specific field of work, and they achieved their goals, because they have that self-belief and positive attitude that you get from loving yourself and appreciating your life.

Know That Everything Is Working Out for You

Knowing you're worthy develops your boldness, and when you're bold and confident, you start to know that everything is working out for you. Then you get even more hopeful, and you get excited; you wake up in the morning and see the world in color, not in black-and-white.

I'm more excited about living now that I've gone through my own transformation. Life is just more amazing because every day, something good happens. I see more good things happening; sometimes it's because there are more good things happening, and other times, it's because I notice the good things that were already there.

I also see more of the good in other people. I love other people more, and good things happen because there are better quality people who are coming into your life. If you have a goal, such as becoming a best-selling author or being a life coach, people that can help you accomplish that dream come into your life, as if it's by magic.

No Matter What You Have Done, You Are Good

It's not what you've done that defines you. That doesn't matter, because you can change your life any time. Start defining yourself by knowing what you want to do, knowing that you can fix your life, and realizing that you can achieve the goals that you want to accomplish in life. Change what you think about your life, and you will change what your life is like.

Work towards reaching the place where you believe you are good. I think everybody is good. When you were born, you were a beautiful little baby: every baby is so beautiful, and when people look at a baby, what do people do? They say, "Oh, wow; so beautiful!" Everybody loves a baby. A baby doesn't know anything yet. And it's worthy of all kinds of love when it's newly born.

What you want to do is reach that place of pure acceptance where even though bad things did happen, you still see yourself as good. Just like when you were a newborn, you're worthy of love simply because you exist. The past is in the past, and you're still good, you're still worthy. You can have whatever you want in life; you just have to decide to let yourself experience that.

Step #10: See the Events & Circumstances of Your Life from a Space of Pure Acceptance

Now you are looking at your life differently, and you're seeing all of the things from the past, all the things that you're living now, and all the things that are possible for your future. You've got a new way of looking at things, a new perspective of the world and your place in it.

Remembering What You Have Done from This Space

Once you've reached the space of pure acceptance, remembering your past doesn't bother you as much, or at all. You've accepted what happened to you and what you've done because of whatever happened, and you learn from it. You even begin to start helping other people. You feel thankful that it did all happen, actually, because you wouldn't be who you are now if those things hadn't happened. Deciding who you're going to be now, along with that perspective of being thankful for who you are today, makes you feel more powerful; it's such a different space to be in.

See That You Weren't Responsible for the Abuse You Experienced

When you give up responsibility for all the things in your

life that you feel were bad and that were holding you back, you find so much freedom from that. You can forgive yourself, forgive others, and move on to a happier life. Whether you have been abused or not, it's time to let go of those past hurts and move forward to a bright, new future.

Shift the Focus from What Doesn't Work

Shift your focus from the past. Before you can accept yourself and get going with the new positivity and happiness in your life, you've always been looking to the past. But you can't drive a car by looking through the rear-view mirror all of the time, and you can't live your life by constantly dwelling in the past. So once you're done with all of what happened to you, and you accept and love yourself, you can move forward in life and really start enjoying the present moment.

Look forward to a new life and a new you. The real you has always been there, but it was hidden. When you live your life as the person who you really are, you will find all of the love, happiness, and peace inside of yourself that you need, and you'll really have fun. Look forward to the things that you want, decide what you want, focus on that, and then you will get the life you've always dreamed of.

You Become Free

It's not that you become free by going through this process; it's the realization that freedom was always there for you. You have your freedom already; you just have to decide to take it. You don't have to be imprisoned, because you had the key to your own freedom the whole time, but you just didn't use it until now. We don't always know how to use it, but the key is always around your neck, waiting to set you free.

This freedom really comes once you allow your emotions to flow unobstructed so that you can reach this space of acceptance. Until you get to this point where you can be okay with feeling and looking at the circumstances in your life without judgment, and just knowing that you are good, you can't possibly forgive another person.

Forgiving others opens a whole new level of freedom in your life. Forgiveness is amazing. It's just so wonderful. The more you do it, the more you can do it. If a person hurts you, you can forgive them right away. You don't waste more time feeling sorry for yourself or feeling anger or whatever it is; you can just forgive right away and keep moving on with your life. Forgiveness is magic to you. Forgive people in your life.

Element #2 Conclusion

As you learned in this element, looking deep inside yourself will not hurt you, and it goes from feeling like, "Oh my god, I think I'm going to die!" to "Okay; just do it! It's going to be okay. You're going to come out the other side; you're going to be able to unlock the door and get out." We'll learn soon how to swing the door open and make all the people who hurt you powerless to hurt you again. You take all the power that you need in your life, without having to put people down or do anything bad, and you can create your own life the way you've always wanted it to be. We are all creators, whether good or bad; we decide.

Later on in this book, we'll be focusing on purging the events and circumstances that hurt you, and then finding out how to discover who you really are, learn to love yourself, and live your life accordingly. Then, finally, we get to focus on building a life of freedom and self-love, which is the best part.

Go to www.LiseLavigne.com/worksheets to download your Choose Your Actions Worksheet before you continue reading.

ELEMENT #3:
Clear the Stuff that Keeps You from Being Who You Really Are; Forgive

"The practice of forgiveness is our most important contribution to the healing of the world."

—Marianne Williamson (author of *A Woman's Worth*)

Welcome to the third critical element of personal transformation. This element is all about letting go of all of the things that have prevented you from being your authentic self and releasing emotional baggage by forgiving those who have hurt you in the past. You might think of it as a "spring cleaning for the soul."

In step #11, you will consider which relationships have helped to shape you, for better or worse. In step #12, you will allow yourself to notice the emotions that come up as you remember these past (or current) relationships. Step #13 will guide you through realizing the effect that these relationships have had on your perception and expression of yourself. Next, in Step #14, contemplate what your life would be like without the emotions that have not been supporting you in your life. Finally, you will progress to step #15, in which you will release the old, bad emotions and make room for the new, good emotions that will bring you peace.

This book is ideal for women who want to change their lives for the better. Critical element #3, "Clear the Stuff That Keeps You from Being Who You Really Are; Forgive," is your personal guide to letting go of the past to be able to prepare for a bright future. We will be following these five steps throughout this third element:

- Step #11: Identify the relationships that have most influenced who you are now

- Step #12: Examine the feelings that thinking about these relationships brings up

- Step #13: See the impact they have on who you think you are

- Step #14: See how your life could be without these feelings

- Step #15: Release your thoughts about these relationships to live with better feelings

Step #11: Identify the Relationships That Have Most Influenced Who You Are Now

This could be positive or negative, but it will probably be mostly negative when you're doing cleanup.

Sit Down Quietly & Trust That You Know

First, create a quiet, safe environment with no distractions: no TV, no music; nothing. When you're ready, sit quietly in a space of trust, and then start thinking about the first memories of whoever it is that hurt you. It could be a situation or it could be a person, but it should be about the cause of the pain that you're still carrying around today.

You need to get in touch with yourself a little bit, and you have to believe that you're in a safe place and that the stuff going on in your head isn't all crazy. Let that start to come to you by sitting down quietly and letting yourself think and feel about what's happened. Just sit and let your thoughts and feelings arise.

Remember Who Hurt You

Sometimes we don't know why we behave a certain way, and we suppress our feelings. We just don't know; it's been so long ago that we don't remember clearly, or we assume it isn't really affecting us anymore, but it is.

Remembering who hurt you brings back the memories of how you felt at that time. If you were always bullied as a child, it could be why you feel afraid of people now; you might think that what happened when you were 7 doesn't matter, but it does matter. It matters because you haven't dealt with it and you're still letting it interfere with your life.

Once you start remembering what happened, you just sit down and you remember everybody who hurt you.

What Was the Abuse—Physical, Emotional, Sexual, or Neglect?

Write down what the person who hurt you did, and how it made you feel at that time (Were you scared? Did it make you feel bad? Did it make you feel guilty?). There can be all kinds of feelings that you had at the time; write all of those down. Those feelings surrounding the abuse and the feelings you have today are related, so when you're able to come to terms with the former, the latter will be easier to deal with. Writing it down can bring up those negative emotions again, so remember to let your feelings flow and remember that it's okay to cry.

Purge All of the Hurt (People, Events, & Circumstances)

Once you've remembered the abuse and how it made you feel, realize that the purpose of doing the purging like this is to let it go. You have to clean it all out. You just can't keep it inside anymore.

Letting go of this is good because holding onto old hurts and bad things that have happened before drags us down in life, even decades later. Sometimes, we remember things being worse than they were, or we assume (without taking the time to remember) that they were worse than they were, so you may actually find that it's not as bad as you think.

Many people internalize the pain that they experienced, and that pain becomes part of their perspective; they learn to fear forming relationships with others, or they learn to be mistrusting of even the people who they've known for years, or they keep a false belief in their mind, such as that "I'm not good now because of what happened to me." You have to let yourself let go of all of that if you want to heal and start living a life of happiness and joy again.

Step #12: Examine the Feelings That Thinking about These Relationships Brings Up

Even thinking about what happened in these relationships is going to bring up a lot of emotions.

Notice How These Harmful Actions Made You Feel

It's important to figure out these emotions because you just have to deal with bad things sometimes. You just have to let it out of your head and out of your heart, because you think about it all the time and it's always there, whether you realize it or not. There's not one day before that I didn't think of the people who hurt me, until I learned to let go of those past hurts.

By really getting into the feelings that these actions caused inside, it freed me from the thoughts of what happened; once it's on paper, it starts to leave your head and your heart because you're letting the emotions flow.

A lot of times, some people don't want to look at what happened. They think that, "If I ignore what happened, it's going to go away," or "I can still live my life if I ignore what happened." Well, no; you can't live like that. You can't just ignore things; you have to deal with what happened so you can move on and be free to live your life.

Release the Impact of Shame

Because you have these bad thoughts every day, you can start to feel really ashamed. But once you start writing down on paper who hurt you, what they did, and how you felt at the time, as an adult you can now start to realize, "Oh, okay: maybe I've felt shame about this, but it's not my fault." Because you're an adult now, you can see things differently and get past what was holding you back.

By experiencing the emotions associated with those hurtful actions, and really letting your emotions flow so that you're releasing it from the heart, the shame doesn't just lessen: it dissipates completely.

Stop Feeling Guilty about the Things That Happened

As you start releasing this shame, you may cry a lot. You finally start to think that it wasn't your fault; you were a child, they were adults, and they had control over you. It wasn't your fault that you were hurt by someone else, even if the abuse happened as an adult. Years later, you start realizing, "Okay, it's not my fault." It releases you from how bad you've been feeling all these years, believing that it was your fault.

How many times did you have to think in your head, "Maybe if I would have done something differently, maybe if I would have had my mom, maybe this wouldn't have happened?" Or any other "If I had…" situation; you could spend hours going through all of the "what if"s and not getting anywhere. You start thinking of all kinds of ways that would have prevented what happened, because you think it's your fault. But once you start writing all of this down, you start to know, "Oh, it's not me." Once it's on paper, you realize, "I had nothing to do with this, man! I didn't know any better, but they knew better." Then you start to release the guilt and shame that you had.

You don't realize overnight that you are good enough. All

these years you felt like, "I'm not good enough, nobody loves me," and you finally realize that it was not true; it was just these people who were doing bad things. The real you has nothing to do with whatever bad things happened to you. Having been hurt doesn't mean you're not good enough, it doesn't mean you're not beautiful, it doesn't mean you're not smart; it doesn't mean any of that. It doesn't mean you were not supposed to be born or that you should kill yourself.

To get to this place, you have to really feel safe enough to let those feelings flow. Creating that safe environment to look at those situations that hurt you and feel the impact that they're having on you today is really transformational. You can start looking at yourself and who you are today, because until you bring awareness to it, you can't see that it does have an impact on you.

Step #13: See the Impact They Have on Who You Think You Are

Your Self-Image Sucks Because of Feeling Inadequate

Your self-image gets obscured when you live all of your life thinking you're not good enough. It affects everything in your life, including your friendships, because when you don't feel lovable or when you don't feel good enough, you can't be who you want to be. When you feel bad, most of the things in your life look bad to you, and that bad attitude brings everyone else down, too.

For example, you might find a good significant other, but because you don't feel good about yourself, you start doing things that will harm the relationship. You find faults with your significant other and start being critical of them because you're critical about yourself, or you don't trust them because you don't feel as though anyone is trustworthy after what happened to you. Your actions are basically driven by the belief that all of the bad things that happened to you will happen again, no matter what, which is why you feel as though you can't trust others anymore.

Feeling Responsible for Everything That Is Bad in Your Life

When you're doing this inner work, you have to start with forgiveness before you do anything else. There's power in letting go by forgiving, and it clears the way to do more.

Once you take a good look at what you've been holding on that has been affecting your life and your perception, you will understand that you need to change. You don't want to live a life obscured by bad feelings from old problems that you're hanging on to. Sometimes, it actually becomes habitual to experience those bad feelings; for example, one person has said about their chronic depression that they were used to being sad and didn't even want to be happy. They were apathetic about the idea of experiencing good emotions on a regular basis. If you let go of those bad feelings, though, not only will you make room for the good emotions to arise, but you will also see how much better it is for you.

Sometimes, we have to change our thought patterns as well to let go of the negativity.

Whether we tell ourselves that we're "ugly," "not good enough," "always going to be poor," or whatever else, we have to realize that it isn't true. Even if those things were true, is that really a reason to not love ourselves? Of course not!

When you start to understand that you are good enough and that you don't have to blame yourself anymore for the bad things that have happened to you, that's when you start thinking differently about everything in your life. When your mind is constantly full of revisiting these incidents from the wrong perspective, it's going to really keep you stuck, but once you let go, you're free.

The Impact of Asking Yourself Questions about What You Should Have Done

Questioning what you should have done in the past is the wrong way to go about it, simply because it doesn't matter what you should have done. If you would have dressed a different way or if you would have done all your homework or whatever else... that kind of thinking only drags you down. Unless you acquire a working time machine and learn the rules of how to avoid creating a time-space paradox, don't waste your time dwelling on what could have been. Bad things happened because of the abusers' issues, not yours. Move on and dwell on what you can become, or simply dwell on the present moment.

What Could Be Different If You Had Done Something Different?

When you keep revisiting this thought: "If I had done something different..." it starts to own you. It's not good to keep wondering about whether it would be different had you done something different, because it drives you absolutely crazy to think about it all the time. It makes you feel guilty because you think it's your fault. Stop feeling guilty, because it's not your fault.

When you go to bed, that thought is always there, and throughout the day, you think about it as well: "I should have done this," or "I should have done that." And then when you grew up, you started having other relationships; you live with a friend or a lover. You think about that as well; say, if the guy hurt you, you're thinking, "Oh my goodness, what have I done? What did I do?" Every time somebody hurts you, you think about that. But you have to stop thinking about it, stop rehashing it over and over in your head of what you should have done, because there's really nothing you can do in the present moment right now to change your past.

Wasting the present moment by thinking about your past and what would be different if you were a different person is totally useless. Instead of shaping tomorrow, you're stuck thinking about whatever happened in the past; yet, even if there were something you could have done differently, it doesn't matter, because you can't go back in a time machine and change it. If they ever invent a time machine, it would probably be either kept entirely secret or time travel would be illegal, so don't count on it!

Step #14: See How Your Life Could Be without These Feelings

Entering the Space of Freedom

When you enter the space of freedom, you have room in your head to start thinking about other things. It's so much

Enough Is Enough!

more peaceful when you stop thinking about things you should not be thinking about, and it's more joyful as well. You can get on with things and you don't procrastinate as much.

When you're more peaceful and joyful and your head is clear, you start living your life differently, in a more peaceful way. People and events around you seem so much more beautiful, and you find more joy in everywhere you go, instead of doom and gloom or stress all of the time.

Stopping the Chatter of These Thoughts in Your Head

Stop that chatter and keep your head clear. If a bad thought starts to enter, say, "No, I'm not going to think like that. That thought is not true." Replace it with something positive instead.

For example, if you want to do something different with your life, like you start thinking of going to Mexico and you want to take Spanish lessons, but then your dad says you're not smart enough, you might automatically think, "Oh, no, he's right: I'm not smart enough. I can't learn a new language." But you can battle that negativity by saying, "No, I AM smart enough. Look at all the things I've done in my life so far!" Your positivity and remembering your achievements counteracts your dad's discouraging comment, and you start looking at your accomplishments that prove that thought is not true. So you basically make sure there's no room for negative chatter by replacing it with evidence of your goodness.

Clearing Space in Your Head

My favorite way of creating space in my head for new things is to just think about the good things, my accomplishments so far, even if they're little. I also love to enjoy the beauty in the world and think about good people that are in my life.

There's always at least one good person in your life; always. There are more good people in your life than bad people, but we sometimes concentrate on the bad and have to remember to focus on the good. Focus on good things, and you will bring even more good things into your life.

Using Your Thoughts to Create Life for Yourself

Your thoughts are creative and can attract good things; you ensure that your thoughts align with the life you want by first deciding what kind of life you want. Do you want this life of being miserable, or do you want a happy, fulfilling life?

You have to decide which life you will choose. If you're at a fork in the road, you choose whether you're going to turn left or turn right. You have to decide; nobody else can do it for you.

You have to decide to do it for your own self. Decide to choose the good, the positive, all the time.

Step #15: Release Your Thoughts about These Relationships to Live with Better Feelings

Let It All Go So It Doesn't Have Any Power Over You Anymore

Stop ruminating about the bad things that have happened in your life. You do need to think about the events that have happened so you can let go, but once you've decided to let go, don't keep coming back to it. You have to say, "Okay, that has happened, I can't do anything about it, and I'm going to forgive whoever did whatever they did."

Revisiting negative events in your life isn't helpful unless you are following the steps towards getting past those events and truly letting go (which means revisiting what happened, forgiving those at fault, forgiving yourself, letting go of old beliefs that were not good, embracing new beliefs that are good, and deciding that you are officially ready to move on—and then no longer ruminating about what happened or labeling yourself as a victim).Don't let them hurt you over and over again by continually rehashing it in your head.

Forgiving those who hurt you doesn't mean that what they did was right or acceptable;it means you're letting them go. It's apiece of luggage you don't have to bring on the plane; you just leave it behind and you don't think about it.

You can let it go because you have dealt with the emotional hole and you can see that you don't want to hold this pain from the past or let it control you. At this point, you've realized that they're like a big weight dragging you down while you're trying to walk. You're dragging one leg behind because of this big weight; once you realize that, you release it and you're free.

Pretend to Be Talking to the People Who Hurt You

Mentally place the people who hurt you in front of you; sometimes you may want to talk to them, but it's not necessary. You just pretend they're in front of you, right there. When you can see them in your mind, say, "This is what you've done to me; this is how I've felt when you did it. I forgive you."

But forgiving does not mean that they had a right to do that or that it was okay for them to do that. That's not what forgiveness means. Most people think it means, "Oh, it's okay what you've done, I'm okay with this." But forgiving is not condoning what they've done.

So you just talk to them and say they are forgiven. Sometimes it's not going to be easy;for example,a lot of times there are people who have passed away and you know they're in heaven. So you say, "Okay, Dad; I forgive you. I want to move on with my own life now. And I'm not going to think about the bad things you've done to me. I forgive you and I'm releasing you." Do that for everybody else, even if you'll never see them again in this life.

Verbalize Your Forgiveness; Make the Statement & Take the Action

When you forgive them, you'll feel like a big weight has been lifted off your shoulder, and it's strange how it happens, but you will start feeling love inside for that person. You feel different, more freedom. You feel like you've had a shower inside of your mind; it really does feel like a cleansing of your spirit and the cleansing of you. It's a new beginning.

Move On with Your Life & Be Free to Be Yourself

This is the best part: you realize that you can have any life that you want. What was holding you back is not there anymore. You can live and think however you want, so your life is yours to create in a good way.

Most of us want a good life. Most of us want to be happy and peaceful and joyful. Will Bowen wrote in his book, "Hurt people hurt people. … People hurt others as a result of their own inner strife and pain…"And it's true: people that are hurting, hurt others. If you stop hurting, then you won't hurt others, because you're not hurting anymore. You have the tools not to hurt others, and you can set them free, too, by forgiving them. That also sets you free.

Element #3 Conclusion

Letting the past remain in the past may take some getting used to, but I can guarantee it will make a difference. If you can't change something, it doesn't make sense to get yourself worked up about it or worrying about it.

The next time someone says something hurtful, consider that they do not necessarily mean to hurt you; as we talked about previously, it could be that they're hurting inside and they don't know how else to express that other than to continue that cycle. Living your life as someone who notices what is going on with themselves and with others means you will more clearly see what is happening and why, which can help to protect you from negativity.

As you learn to love yourself and become the person who you were always meant to be, you will naturally become more empathetic and compassionate of others. Remember that we are all going through our own struggles—some of which we may believe *nobody else* ever goes through—and that even something as simple as being friendly or having a kind attitude can lift others up.

Read the next element to learn more about what it takes to unconditionally love yourself.

Go to www.LiseLavigne.com/worksheets to download your Letting Go of Hurt Worksheet before you continue reading.

ELEMENT #4:
Discover Who You Really Are; Start Loving Yourself

> "To the people who love you, you are beautiful already. This is not because they're blind to your shortcomings but because they so clearly see your soul. Your shortcomings then dim by comparison. The people who care about you are willing to let you be imperfect and beautiful, too."
>
> —Victoria Moran (author of *Lit from Within: Tending Your Soul for Lifelong Beauty*)

Welcome to the fourth critical element of personal transformation. This element is all about discovering your authentic self and beginning to love yourself despite any events of the past. As you learn to love yourself just as you are, you will find that your love for others grows, too, and your life will be more harmonious. You will also become your own ally and advocate, having the self-worth to protect yourself from dangerous situations or abusive people.

In step #16, you will decide to quit doing the things that you think others expect of you (but that you don't really like).

In step #17, you will discover your hobbies and interests independent of what the crowd thinks is cool; you will start to find out what makes you happy. Step #18 will guide you through fully enjoying that happiness that comes from doing what you really want. Next, in step #19, you will see and bask in your own inner goodness—yes, I said "bask"! Finally, in step #20, you will find out what your hidden talents are and how you can use them to make a better life for yourself.

This book is ideal for women who want to change their lives for the better. Critical element #4, "Discover Who You Really Are; Start Loving Yourself," is your personal guide to being your own best friend and treating yourself with the loving kindness that you deserve. We will be following these five steps throughout this fourth element:

- Step #16: Stop doing all the things you think you should do
- Step #17: Do something you think you want or like; anything
- Step #18: Learn to find inner enjoyment in what you're doing
- Step #19: Experience your goodness
- Step #20: Let your inner gifts reveal themselves to you

Step #16: Stop Doing All the Things You Think You Should Do

Here, we're really talking about the thoughts, the social conditioning, the norms, and what the hurt does.

Stop Pleasing Others

Decide to stop pleasing others. If people expect you to bitch and complain, and that's going to hurt you, you're just not going to do it; you're not going to be involved in anything like that, because it doesn't really make you happy. So you can give an excuse, "I'm sorry; I forgot to do something," and just leave. You don't want to get into those conversations, you don't want to talk about negative things; you want to be positive. Don't do something you are against just to be liked.

Remove yourself from bad situations. A lot of people expect you to participate in their conversations, even when they're speaking of bad things, and maybe the old you would have just joined in because it would have made them happy. But you have to decide what you want and don't want, and then you have to just go for it.

Stop Doing Things That Are Detrimental to You

When you start having this level of awareness, you begin noticing that your negative thoughts are detrimental to you. If you hang out with people who constantly talk about bad things, those thoughts can easily come into your own mind.

Remind yourself, "No, what they're talking about isn't true." Don't listen to what they have to say; stay away from gossip and negativity. To keep your thoughts supporting you, you have to counteract those thoughts with other good thoughts; the more you think of good things, the easier it will be to lead a good life.

Never Sacrifice What You Believe In

Believe that you are good, you are lovable, your life is going to be great, and this world can be great (or is great).

When things are happening that go against your beliefs, it's very hard, but it's doable. You can do it. You can just say, "No, I'm sorry, I don't believe that," or you can say, "No, I don't want to talk about that." You can say why, and eventually, you stop hanging out with those people. Sometimes, they will leave your life entirely.

There's a person who used to be in my life but isn't anymore. She wasn't good for me; she was always talking about her life in a negative way and it was always attracting bad circumstances to her life. She had so many boyfriends but broke up with them fast. She was always complaining, even when things were going well. It was painful being around that kind of negativity. When I became a more positive, happy person, she was no longer in my life.

The same thing will happen to you: as you become more positive and happy, that kind of people will start showing up in your life. Eventually, you just find new friends. New people come to you. That's what's been happening to me.

Ask Yourself, "Is It Me Who Wants to Do This? Is This Part of Who I Am?"

Most people live their life without really thinking about anything, it seems; they just get up in the morning, they go to work, and then they come home and they watch reality TV shows that don't add anything to one's life, such as "The Bachelor," "The Bachelorette," or "Big Brother." And all they talk about are those stupid shows. It doesn't really add anything to your life; it really doesn't.

If people are encouraging you to adopt the same kind of lifestyle as them, you should first ask yourself if the real you wants to do that and if it aligns with your true self. Don't get involved in things that aren't going to make you happy or that make you feel as though you're wasting your life. Look for activities and people that bring happiness and joy to your life.

Step #17: Do Something You Think You Want or Like; Anything

Sometimes it can be so hard when you're so used to interacting with the same people and you're used to being part of the crowd to even find out what you like, but you can do it.

Remember Things That You Thought You Wanted to Do or Try

Maybe you've always wanted to try to learn tennis. As a kid, you wanted to learn tennis, or go roller blading, and now's the time. It doesn't matter how old you are; you can always try it. It's not as if you're going to break a leg. You can try it and you might love it, and you might be good at it, too.

Or you might just want to explore your own city because you've never done it before because you were always hanging out with the wrong crowd or you were always working.

Make it a habit to try new things, even if it's as simple as trying out a new restaurant. There are so many activities out there; take a leap of faith to try just one thing that you want to do. Then you'll have so much fun that you'll seek out even more things that you really want to do.

Ask a Friend or Take a Class

Luckily for us, we now have this wonderful thing called Meetup. And you can go online, and there are hundreds and hundreds of different subjects of Meetup groups. That's another great way of meeting people.

If you join the group, you can do different activities together, which is great because some people don't want to do anything all by themselves. Being in that group of people might be better for them. Try anything, get yourself doing things that are new; something different, unfamiliar, out of the box.

Start to Develop Your Own Likes & Dislikes

Once you start doing something, you'll find that other people are coming to you. You can develop new friendships. I found that when I go to the gym, people come up to me and start a conversation,and then we find we have things in common.

The other day, I went to a workshop, with only women there, and I found my next best friend there! She's just amazing! She really is. She's having trouble in her life, but she is just an amazing person with a great attitude.

Develop yourself, start knowing who you are by trying new activities, and then new friendships will come along, even at work: new staff come in, and you find out that, "Oh, look at how much in common we have!"

Enjoy Your Exploration of Yourself, & the World Opens Up to You

Once you start trying these new things you've never done before that you've always wanted to do, you start liking it and you do more and more of it. You want to experience even more, so you try something else or you go even deeper into that activity to enjoy. You might become better at it. If you love tennis, for example, you might want to take more lessons and develop your talent, and who knows? You might become a champion.

At this point, you find that you get excited about life, and you even want to try new things. The people in your life are so much better, your conversations are better, your energy level gets higher, and you feel so much happier. It becomes harder and harder for bad things that happen to take control of your life, because you're living higher than your circumstances, and people can't bring you down anymore. You won't let them.

Step #18:   Learn to Find Inner Enjoyment in What You're Doing

So many of us think that we have to do things to cause enjoyment, and we're finding that that's just not true. We can find joy in the present moment, even if it's as simple as being thankful for being alive and being well. Always find reasons to be grateful. Start each day being thankful for your life and end each day by finding good things to be thankful for.

Take in the Environment

I love nature. Right now, I'm looking at the view I have, and I see the train, I see some cars, and I see a big park in front of me. The colors are just so beautiful; so many different shades of green.

And then you start to think about the wonder of it all. Like, how did it grow? Almost every leaf is different.

By taking in the environment around you, you just enjoy nature a lot more. It's so much fun to watch the ducks in the pond, just relax, and look at the beauty of those ducks. Or you can just sit quietly on a chair with your own thoughts and appreciate everything that you have so far: no matter what's going on, you're still breathing. There is so much more goodness than that to appreciate, and there will always be a lot of good in the world.

Appreciate What You're Doing & How Much You'll Enjoy It

Try new things, and most of the time, you'll find that it's fun, even if you don't do it ever again. Once, I tried bowling, and I was surprised to find that it was fun. I never thought bowling would be fun, because it looks so stupid and boring on TV, but it really was fun. It wasn't just the activity itself, but the energy level of the people around me; we were all having such an enjoyable time.

When you do things with other people who are enjoying what they're doing, you start enjoying it, too, even if you're never going to do it ever again.

I've also tried curling once, too. It was a work event, and I said, "Okay, I'll go with you guys." I never thought I would enjoy that. You might think you look silly while you curl, but I had so much fun doing it! Again, it's because the energy level is just so high, and people are enjoying what they're doing or enjoying the company of each other, and it's just so much fun.

Watch What Kind of People Show Up Around You

It seems like when your life is fun and when your attitude is wonderful, you find more and more people with that kind of attitude coming into your life. When you're enjoying life, you find the people around you start to show another side of themselves.

Just last week, at work, I saw someone who I always thought was a little bit unhappy. I had kept trying to show the real me when I was around her: I try to be happy all the time and find the good in people. Now I'm seeing another side of her that I've never seen before. She smiles more, and she actually giggled the other day. I don't know whether she's trusting me more or what happened there, but the good part of her is starting to show.

Create a List of Things You Like

If you keep doing things that you like, it gives you more energy. You look forward to getting up in the morning instead of waking up grumpy and wondering, "Is it 7 o'clock already? Oh, no! I have to do all these things today…"

When you enjoy your life, your activities, and the people around, you get up and it gives you a level of energy you've never had before. There's no need for coffee to wake you up. I still drink coffee, because I do love the taste, but it's not as if I think, "I need my coffee because I can't get through today without my coffee. I just can't live without it."

You get excited about life, even the little things: "Oh, wow; I get to do this today! At 3 o'clock, I'm having coffee with so-and-so." Or, "At 12, I'm going to have lunch with my favorite friend." Or, "Oh, yeah; I have this lawyer I have to talk to.

Looking forward to that meeting." Your activities in your life become more enjoyable, they make you happier. It's much better to live this way.

Step #19: Experience Your Goodness

Know You Are Doing Things You Believe In

Doing what you believe in makes your life different because you're actually being true to yourself. You won't resort to things that will not make you happy or that will make you feel all those bad things you used to feel, such as guilt, anger, frustration, and uneasiness.

When you're true to yourself and you do the things that you want to do, you become more joyful and more confident. You have a new outlook on life. You see the thousands of possibilities out there.

You don't look at your life and think, "Oh, my gosh; this is what I'm supposed to be doing in my life?" with everything looking so gloomy. No; it opens up all of these new possibilities.

Your attitude towards people changes, you love them more, and you even love strangers more because you feel so much more happiness inside. You really do. You feel love for people in a way that you've never experienced before. It's a good, healthy love.

Do Things Because You Want to & Because They Align with Your True Self

I believe that the true person inside was always there, but

bad things have happened and we've let those things happen to us, and our thoughts, our bad thoughts were in our way. Now that the real you has shown up, it's just magical.

You want to make sure the things you do align with that self, because that's where true happiness comes from. Living in alignment with your true self is one of the secrets to happiness.

Look for Good Feedback; Observe the Good Feelings That You Get

This is really a way to find out if what you're doing is aligned with your true self. I have found that people comment on the changes that are happening in your life. Many people say, "You're not who you used to be. Years ago, you would not think like that. You're so adventurous now! You're so busy now; you have a real life." Some people come to you for advice in their own lives, and then you hear all kinds of compliments from people that you didn't hear before.

Let the Guilt, Shame, & Love Be the Indicators That You're on the Right Track; Experience the Peace

Your emotions can guide you. I had lunch yesterday to celebrate a friend's birthday, and I didn't want to go at first because I knew where the conversation would go. But I went because it was this woman's birthday and I wanted to celebrate her. We went to lunch, and I talked about good things, but then the conversation started to lead elsewhere, and I felt yucky inside—I just felt like I had fallen into a puddle of mud.

I knew I was not supposed to listen to this; I was not supposed to be there. I did not want to be part of what was going on right then. My gut feeling told me, "Okay, this is not the place you're supposed to be or what you're supposed to listen to."

I tried to change the subject, and eventually, the lunch ended, thank goodness. I wasn't really able to turn everything around, but you feel it in your heart. Sometimes it's a thought: "No, Lise; you're not supposed to do that," or, "No, Lise; go away. Don't do that." Sometimes it's a feeling inside, and you have to trust that.

The times that I haven't trusted my intuition and have gone against it, I have not been happy afterwards. So you always have to trust what's inside of you. Some experts say, "The answer is within you." Well, that's true! The answer is within you; you just have to tap into it. To me, intuition is God's spirit, but that's a subject for another book.

Step #20: Let Your Gifts Reveal Themselves to You

Find a Community Where You Can Show Up Regularly

We need to hang out with others; as human beings, we need each other. Many times, people hang out with the wrong crowd. When you hang out with a good crowd that aligns with your own self, it makes you even better. It makes you believe that you can do anything, and it gives you confidence and happiness. It gives positive energy.

Those people see our true gifts and we all share our gifts together. So when you find a good group of people, that's what happens. I go to church and I like the group there; you might find a good group at church, at work, or while swimming or engaging in some other hobby where you can meet people.

Interact with People and Be Your True Self

Interact with people and don't be afraid to be hurt by others. Share your life with your friends and other people, and just keep looking for friends. Keep looking for people who align with your true self. They're out there. Most of the time, you won't even have to look for them; they'll just show up.

Watch for How People Start to Show Up for You

People just start showing up. You could be having coffee at Starbucks, for example, and have a conversation with somebody while you're waiting in line. I'm starting out as a life coach, and I'm seeing that other people need me in their life; they want me to coach them on improving their lives, and I love that I can help them.

It's just like magic. It happens when you feel good about yourself and you surround yourself with good things, good vibrations. When you vibe right, on a higher level, people at that higher level come into your life automatically. You attract them.

I went to a simple workshop and I found the most amazing friend, Michelle. She's my next best friend. Who knew I would have found her there, at a workshop, of all places? But I found her, even though I wasn't looking for her. I knew I needed a real, true girlfriend to talk to about anything, and I found her just by going to a workshop.

Let Others Show You What They Value Most in You

The people in your life will value the real person that you are, and they'll want to be with you because you're valuable to them. Maybe you bring them happiness or peace or make them feel good about themselves when they're with you. They want to be with you, and most of the time, they will tell you that.

I've found that the people with high vibrations are easier to talk to. They're more open than others, and they just appreciate things in life more. They appreciate you and express that appreciation, which makes you feel really good about yourself.

You can find your own gifts by what others tell you; they might say, "You're so easy to talk to; you're always listening. You're always so positive. You've been through all that hell and you've come out of it, now look at you!"

I thought I was nobody for a long time, and that I was an accident—that's what my dad used to say, because my mom didn't want to give birth to me. But I was born anyway, and here I am. And I'm not stopping. I want to help people.

I thought I had no gifts. But now, I'm so much more than what I used to think about myself. Now, people think I'm classy and I have style. I can help people; I can make people happy. I can change people's lives. I can listen to them and have fun with them. They come to me for advice, and I love my new path as a life coach.

Element #4 Conclusion

Embracing your individuality and focusing on your inner talents can increase your feelings of empowerment and self-worth. Dare to be yourself despite what you think others might think of you. Your inherent worth will shine when you are following the right life path for you, whether that means finding a relationship with God, switching to a more uplifting career, nourishing your soul by regularly connecting with nature, or anything else that brings joy into your life. You are worth much more than you know, and once you have a good circle of friends, they will be there to lift you up when you need them. As you progress to the final element of this book, I want to encourage you to start living your best life. Read on to find out exactly how to build the life that you have always dreamed of living.

Go to www.LiseLavigne.com/worksheets to download your Opening to New Possibilities Worksheet before you continue reading.

ELEMENT #5:
Build The Life You Want From a Place of Freedom & Self-Love

> *"The future belongs to those who believe in the beauty of their dreams."*
>
> —Eleanor Roosevelt (civil rights advocate)

Welcome to the fifth critical element of personal transformation. This element is all about moving on to create a life of prosperity and happiness. Your confidence, self-esteem, self-love, and the positive emotions you have been nourishing will flourish and guide you throughout the rest of your life.

In step #21, you will listen to the intuitive feelings that arise to nudge you in the right direction for a better, healthier lifestyle in which you put yourself first. In step #22, you will put your faith in something bigger than yourself and put your plans for change into action. Step #23 gives you the perfect chance to meet new people as the "new you" and form meaningful, healthy relationships with others. Next, in step #24, you will remember to appreciate the inspiration that now guides you in your life. Finally, in step #25, you will receive the tools to create a good life for yourself that will make you happy.

This book is ideal for women who want to change their lives for the better. Critical element #5, "Build the Life You Want from a Place of Freedom & Self-Love," is your personal guide to creating the reality that you have always dreamed of and fulfilling your divine destiny. We will be following these five steps throughout this fifth element:

- Step #21: Ask to have your path revealed to you
- Step #22: Trust that what shows up is right
- Step #23: Share who you are with others
- Step #24: Revel as what you are here to do is revealed to you
- Step #25: Build your life from knowing that you are on the right path

Step #21:   Ask to Have Your Path Revealed to You

The truth is, you're always on the path and it's always there for you; it's just a matter of whether you're seeing it.

Know That You Have a Purpose in Your Life That You Want to Find

Everybody is born with a purpose. You're not created just to crawl on the road. You have a purpose, whether you know it or not. A lot of us don't know what it is, especially after the kind of life we've had, where we've felt unloved and unwanted and useless. Once you come out of all of that junk, though, your good qualities come out, and so does the real you.

If you're focused on all the people around you and the things that are hurting you, it can keep you from seeing that you have a purpose. Once that is all gone, you're free from all of that. Then you start doing the things you like and associating with people whose company you enjoy. People start telling you what you're good at. They say, "Oh, you're a great listener," or "Oh, I didn't know you had that talent; you should pursue that."

I didn't know what my purpose was for a long time, and most of my life, I thought I was supposed to be rich. I thought, "Maybe I'll marry a rich man." I didn't marry a rich man, but I did discover what my true purpose in life was, which is a lot better anyway.

I asked God to show me what my purpose is because I didn't know. I even took some personality and talent tests, and I still couldn't figure out what I was good for. The tests showed I was good at several different things, but then I had no clue how to put it all together. I still wondered, "What am I supposed to do with my life? I still don't know. So what if I'm good at listening or I'm good at encouraging people and serving people and helping, and all that; I still do not know."

But now I'm finding out that I want to become a successful life coach rather than working as a paralegal, and the more that I get involved in that, the happier I become. I'm not just preparing court documents anymore or doing other things to assist lawyers; now I make a real difference in people's lives by providing coaching for them, and I get to see them turn their lives around. It's wonderful.

Ask a Greater Knowing What You Are Here to Do

When you ask the higher power, "Please reveal to me my purpose; what did you make me for? How can you use me?

Show me," it doesn't take long. All of the sudden, things happen. It's like magic.

For example, I went through the Freedom Session Program to figure out why I was attracting all of these bad relationships in my life. That's what helped me to become who I am now. They asked me if I wanted to be a sponsor to other women; I said, "Okay; that's fine, I can do that." It's easy; you just listen to them and be there for them when they call you at all hours of the day. I just loved doing it, and I loved being appreciated for being there for them. They were even bragging to other people about me, which further showed that they really appreciated my help.

The lady in charge of the women's ministry then asked me if I wanted to be a mentor at a safe house through Salvation Army to some women who had been abused. I said, "Sure! I'll do that." So I did that, and I just found that I loved it. I loved listening and encouraging the women there. Then I was asked again to help out at another safe house and share my story to encourage them.

Basically, God put people in my life who asked me to do things that I actually said "yes" to, that I thought I would like. That's how I discovered my purpose in life. My purpose is to help women with a similar background to mine.

Sponsor Freedom in Another Person

Because I know what I've been through, I know how I came out of it, and I know the difference of how I felt even just five years ago, I want to help other people have that same transformation. I want people to find the same peace and freedom inside that I feel now, with my life so different from how it was.

When I'm able to help other people to see the light, get over the fears that they have, and help them move forward in life, it just touches me so deeply that I can help people. I feel like, "Oh, I have a purpose!" You can feel the same way, too. You can find your own purpose.

Look for the Things That Are Right in Front of You, Showing You the Way

The path is laid out for you once you ask. As you follow your intuition and invite good things into your life, you will find that things start getting so much better for you. You will find that there are so many good things in your life that you even have prayers that are nothing more than "thank you"s to God or the Universe or whatever you call your Higher Power.

Step #22: Trust That What Shows Up Is Right

Let Things Start to Show Up Magically

Magic is a trick, usually; you go see a magician, and it's all trickery. It feels wonderful, it looks wonderful, but it's all tricks. This transformation feels like magic, but the difference is this is real, because it does happen. Good things really do start to show up in your life, and you get that same sense of it all feeling wonderful. You can't believe the way your life is turning out, because it's so radically different from what you're used to.

Good people show up in your life, and then what happens is when the real you starts to show up, you can actually feel it because you notice the difference between the things you would do before and what you do now.

When you're in a bad situation, for example, it's, "Oh, I'm

not going to do that." The real you shows up by you deciding, "Oh, I'm not going to do that," or "Yes, I will do that; that sounds good." When it happens, you actually notice that, "Before, you wouldn't have chosen that, Lise," or, "You would not have said that, Lise." The real person is now actually showing up, and you actually notice a difference.

Look to the Things That You've Always Wanted to Do

The things I wanted to do are happening. I never knew what I wanted to do, exactly, but I knew some of the things I wanted: to be happier, more confident, stop being afraid, and find good people who I could trust and have good relationships with. I wanted to do good things with my life; useful things. I didn't want to just be a toy for guys. I wanted to do something with my life; at 50 years old, you have to!

Things that I thought were like a dream started being realized. I'm at the beginning of my big dream, and it's only getting better.

Start to See the Opportunities That Show Up in Your Awareness

I started seeing more opportunities because I changed myself. Maybe the opportunities were always there, but I didn't see them before.

For example, I know that I was always trying to help people. Sometimes I was helping people in a bad way, like when I was doing things I didn't want to do, thinking I was going to make them happy, and it didn't make either of us happy although I was trying to help them.

People would come to me, sometimes; in the old days, my friends would come to me and ask for my advice. I knew

I always wanted to help them. Looking back at it now, I know I was supposed to be helping people. But now, because I think differently, I live differently, and I'm a different person completely, it's almost like the universe is bringing me all of these opportunities. And I see those opportunities and use them.

Seize the Opportunities That Present Themselves

If I see or hear something that has to do with my purpose, I just grab onto it. I don't really ask questions now; I just grab onto it and I run with it.

Last week, Paul asked me, "Have you ever thought of joining ToastMasters?" I had gone there as a guest about two years ago and never did anything about it because I was scared. Bob had said to go to ToastMasters if I wanted to be a best-selling author. I went but never did anything about it because I still had that fear inside of me. Now, though, I feel as if everything is coming together with my purpose. So I said, "Yeah! I have to do that!" As soon as I got to the office, I emailed Royalty Toast-Masters, and I told them, "Next Wednesday, I'm going to join. I've been there as a guest a few times, but I am now joining. No more fear anymore; I'm doing this."

You might have a different purpose than me; your purpose might be to be a famous guitar-player, or whatever else, but mine is to help women. Whatever your purpose is, take the opportunities that come with it.

Step #23:   Share Who You Are with Others

Watch Who Starts to Show Up Naturally

Notice what starts to show up in yourself (how you change

internally). The real you is showing up, and you can see how different it is from who you used to be. Then, notice people who start to show up naturally in your life. It's amazing when I think of the people who have showed up in my life. Bob, my publisher, showed up again in my life three years later, and I don't believe that's a coincidence. I don't believe in coincidences anymore. Everything happens for a reason.

A few months ago, a friend of mine was telling me how she became friends with a national television host. Then, a few weeks later, my friend invited me to participate in that host's new talk show. They were taping a few episodes to be aired soon. I jumped at this opportunity because one of my dreams is to one day be on television helping millions of women.

Find the Good Emotions & Let Them Guide What You Do

As minimal as my part was, being involved in this new television series gave me great hope. It was an honor to be there and meet a wonderful celebrity. She doesn't know this, but I even sat on her makeup chair and declared, "One day, it will be my turn. I will be on television." Each time I see her television show, it reminds me that I talked to that lady and even hugged her.

I hope that one day she remembers what we talked about, and that she invites me to share my story on her show. Knowing that this meeting I had with her could be an open door to be on television is exciting, and it gives me the energy and strength to move on with every step of my work. Meanwhile, I help as many women as I possibly can until that day comes.

Enough Is Enough!

Fill Yourself Up & Serve from a Place of Wholeness

Now you're giving to other people, but not to try to get someone to love you; now you're giving because you're overflowing with joy and other good emotions. You have something to give now, because you're not empty inside. You don't have all these bad things inside that are keeping you from people and from your purpose, and you actually have love to give now; real love and real peace to give.

Help People from a Place That Energizes You

When I see people who are hurting, and I know what they've been through and I know I can help them, I just give them my best. I used to do anything for anybody, which made me feel worse. Now, it's different; when I give to somebody, and I see some changes in them—even if it's just a smile or a glance of hope in their life—it just makes me feel so good and useful. I have healthy boundaries now and I'm empowered by what I'm doing, because I've helped somebody in a good way. Their life is positive and my life is positive. I give, I help, but I still have a lot to give, and I keep on giving. I don't run out of love and courage to give, and I don't feel shame about it, because it's all healthy.

Step #24: Revel as What You Are Here to Do Is Revealed to You

Life Is Really Different, & You Feel Really Good

There's a really neat transformation that starts happening as you're on your path and you're seeking your purpose. For example, people are actually asking for my business cards. I tell them, "I'm a life coach now, and I have these business cards." I'm bragging to my co-workers, and they want my business cards because they want to give them to other people. It feels so good to think that people actually notice that I have some value to give to others.

Goals Start to Become Easy to Set, & You Know You Will Do Anything to Get It Done

Setting goals give you a certain kind of energy inside; we feel passion, like we're on fire or something. We just keep on moving.

I have two jobs now: my job during the day is for one purpose, and then my job during the night is for a different purpose. I have different energy at night because it's for a different purpose. It's for my book, and it's to payoff debts. Everything I do now is to reach my ultimate goal.

Sometimes I get tired, but it doesn't take long before I feel energized again because I'm doing this, and nothing is going to stop me. I know what I'm doing. It's very energetic.

See How the Whole Universe Is Conspiring to Make Your Dreams Come True

It almost feels as if the whole universe really is conspiring to make your dreams come true. I've seen that in my own life: the events, circumstances, people, and the conversations that I've been having... I feel as though I'm the only person in this world.

I go to Chapters and I see all of these books to help me with my business. I say, "Oh my gosh, this is going to be helpful for my clients!" or "This is going to be helpful for me." It's just so good. The people who are showing up, they're all about to help me with my purpose. I just feel wonderful.

Trust That Your Life Can Be Exactly As You Want It to Be

You have to trust that your life can be what you want it to be and really believe that, because it's true. I never thought before that I would be happy without a man in my life; I always had a man in my life, even if it was just for one night. Now, I haven't had a man in my life for about five years! And it's not because I don't attract them; even on Sunday, I could have had a man in my life, but I said no.

Life can be the way you want it. Right now, I'm working on myself and my new career, and that's all that matters right now. You can be happy doing whatever it is that is your purpose; you can achieve your goals and be happy doing that.

Step #25: Build Your Life from Knowing That You Are on the Right Path

Wake Up in the Morning with Eagerness for the Day

Wake up and see what happens during the day. Ask God, "What do you have for me today, Lord?" You can call him anything you want, but you just ask, and people will show up. Things will happen. It's amazing. God does listen to us. He just wants us to talk to him.

Being eager in the morning when you wake up means you feel really alive. You're not just surviving anymore. You're not just living day to day, doing the same things over and over again with no meaning. Now everything is joyful. Everything is loving and so powerful.

Everything you do is better. Everything you taste, tastes better. A cup of coffee, just a simple cup of coffee in the morning, tastes better because you see things differently from what you used to see. You feel differently than what you used to feel. It's as if you're on fire every morning with your passion for life that you never had before.

Let the Day Be Exciting & Joyful

Start your day on good footing. When I wake up early for a reason, like a phone call I have to take, I'm not a morning person. I feel groggy and all of that, but I am still happy inside because I know that that grogginess will go away, and I just feel energized, even though I'm tired.

Life is so much better now when you wake up in the morning because you know what your life is, you know what you're supposed to be doing, you know what you like, you know who you are, you know what you want to do, you have goals, and you're not letting anything stop you from doing anything.

Know That Every Day You Are Closer to the Goal; Everything Else Is Just Temporary

Think of the big picture and what the end goal of it is. Everything else is just temporary until you reach your goal. When you reach that goal, you might have another goal that you can focus on. Keep your sights set on where you're going, and you will know that what you're living is just steps along the way; that's all it is.

It's easier when you keep the big picture in your head; it's easier to accept the temporary circumstances, because you know, "Oh, that's going to change soon." Like, "Oh, I'm not going to be doing this kind of work forever, so it's okay if I have to do this boring job." It's only temporary. It makes you see your present circumstances better, more positively.

Live Inspired in Your Big Dreams, & Feel the Difference in Your Body from Being Happy All the Time

Even though you may be tired from all the work you're doing, you focus on your happiness and your goal. You're energized and that tiredness dissipates. When you know what your purpose is and you know what your goals are, it gives you this energy and your body actually feels different.

Personally, it makes me feel tingling inside; it's so exciting and wonderful. That keeps me in that state of joy, and people see that. At work, people don't understand why I'm so happy; they just don't understand. They say, "Lise is always happy." "Lise is so nice." "You have a problem? Go see Lise. She'll help you." People really notice the difference.

Anywhere you are in your life, no matter how it looks or how bad you see it, you can get to a place where you live inspired. You just have to change your mind and believe that it is possible to be happy all the time, because it is. It is absolutely possible to be happy all the time if you choose. You just have to choose to be happy.

It's a knowing. And that knowing is very powerful; that's the absolute of your outcome, because of that knowing. There will be no other outcome. Getting to that place of knowing is hard work, but when you get there, there's nothing like it, and it's amazing.

Element #5 Conclusion

If you haven't already, now is the time to get started chasing your dreams! There is so much wonder and light in our lives; go out there and explore it. Now that you've found your freedom, think about going on an adventure of your lifetime. What have you always wanted to do with your life but have never done because you lacked the self-confidence or thought others wouldn't approve? Go out and do it!

The more you live the life you've always secretly wanted for yourself, the happier you will become and the better you will feel about yourself. Every single one of us has to make the choice between a negative or positive action, no matter what our circumstances are. I plead with you to choose a positive action.

You don't have to travel the world, climb mountains, or make an amazing scientific discovery to start living the life you really want; even something small like joining a book club or meeting someone new can give your life the enthusiasm and spirit that you've been wanting. Live life for yourself, and who knows? You could even write a book. I did it, and so can you!

Go to www.LiseLavigne.com/worksheets to download your Discover & Express Your Gifts Worksheet.

CONCLUSION

Living life for yourself is something that you may have only ever dreamed of before, yet, if you follow the suggestions in this book for personal transformation, it is something you can reach. (You could already be doing it right now!) In this book, you have discovered the five critical elements to becoming a strong, independent, empowered woman:

- Element #1: Develop the trust that looking deep inside yourself will not hurt you

- Element #2: Let yourself see the events that hurt or disempowered you; let the feelings flow

- Element #3: Clear the stuff that keeps you from being who you really are; forgive

- Element #4: Discover who you really are; start loving yourself

- Element #5: Build the life you want from a place of freedom & self-love

In the first element, you began your soul work of discovering what's going on with your emotions, why you're living the way that you are, and your potential for adopting a healthier life and outlook.

In the second element, you started to accept what happened to you in the past and experienced the bottled-up emotions that had been preventing you from moving forward.

In the third element, you worked to let go of your façade that came from pleasing others and replaced it with your genuine self. You also freed your heart through forgiving those who had hurt you in the past.

In the fourth element, you promised yourself that you would begin to cultivate unconditional self-love and treat yourself with the respect that you deserve. You also discovered the interests, skills, and activities that bring you joy and happiness.

In the fifth element, you began to create a good life in which you are safe, healthy, happy, and are emotionally balanced. You also began to live in the moment and chase your dreams.

That's a huge transformation, and I think you should be proud of yourself. No matter how long your journey of becoming emotionally free from the past and learning to love yourself, I'm sure you'll agree that it was definitely worth it.

As you go forward in your life, I encourage you to seek out other women who have had similar problems in their lives and let them know that you're there for them and that you support them. Whenever you find yourself falling into the same negative thought patterns of the past or wishing that your life would somehow instantly fix itself, I want to encourage you to find a way to help someone else in their life. Life is never as difficult when we are surrounded by friends or engaged in a good cause. Make it a habit to help others, especially those who cannot ask for help or whose pride prevents them from speaking up. Freely share your love with others, and your life will be blessed. Remember, if you change your mind, you change your life.

Wishing you prosperity and happiness,

Lise

RESOURCES

EMERGENCY SERVICES

Suicide Prevention
Phone: 1-800-SUICIDE (1-800-784-2433)
Phone: 1-800-273-TALK (1-800-273-8255)
Website: www.Suicide.org

YWCA Canada Women's & Children's Shelter Directory
Phone:(416) 962-8881
Website: http://YWCACanada.ca/en/pages/national/associations (available in English and Français)
This directory lists shelters all across Canada (including the one listed below): Alberta, British Columbia, Manitoba, New Brunswick, Newfoundland, Nova Scotia, Northwest Territories, Nanuvut, Ontario, Quebec, and Saskatchewan.